Kingdom Publishers

When God Made the World

Copyright©Sheela Burrell

All rights reserved. No part of this book may be reproduced in any form by photocopying or any electronic or mechanical means, including information storage or retrieval systems, without permission in writing from both the copyright owner and the publisher of the book. The right of Sheela Burrell to be identified as the author of this work has been asserted by her in accordance with the Copyright, Designs and Patents Act 1988 and any subsequent amendments thereto.

A catalogue record for this book is available from the British Library.

All Scripture Quotations have been taken from the NIV.

ISBN: 978-1-911697-84-8

1st Edition by

Kingdom Publishers,

London, UK.

You can purchase copies of this book from any leading bookstore or email contact@kingdompublishers.co.uk

This book belongs to

....

"For all the children in the world, young or old, tall or short and big or small."

In the beginning, God created the heavens and the earth. Genesis 1:1

When God Made the World

When God made the world, He made a special place. It was a brand new planet that dazzled, shone and sparkled.

When God made the world, He pinned planets and galaxies in space and hung stars that flickered like fireflies far away.

When God made the world, He took out His paintbox and splashed green, blue, red, pink, yellow, orange and purple. Out came flowers, trees, birds and butterflies.

When God made the world, He whispered, and the oceans came alive with all sorts of fish and animals. There were whales in the water, turtles and trout and sea creatures in the deep.

When God made the world, He created lions, zebras, giraffes, and even tiny hedgehogs.

When God made the world, He was not alone. His Son was with Him. Together, they scooped up the earth and made children.

When the world was complete, God was happy. He sang and danced because the world looked amazing! It was a masterpiece!

But one day, darkness came like a silent mist and covered the earth. It grew bigger and bigger. The children were sad. They were scared and lost.

"Who will help the children?" God asked.

"I will go," the Son said.

So Jesus, God's Son, came to earth to help the children. He came as a little baby born in a manger. The night Jesus was born, the angels sang, the shepherds rejoiced and light came into the world.

Jesus is God's special gift to the world. He is the light of the world who came to take darkness away forever.

This is not the end.

This is only the beginning.

God's story continues...

For God so loved the world that he gave his one and only Son...
John 3:16

www.ingramcontent.com/pod-product-compliance
Lightning Source LLC
Chambersburg PA
CBHW041503220426
43661CB00016B/1240